V.
HONOR YOUR FATHER AND YOUR MOTHER.

VI.
YOU SHALL NOT KILL.

VII.
YOU SHALL NOT COMMIT ADULTERY.

VIII.
YOU SHALL NOT STEAL.

IX.
YOU SHALL NOT BEAR FALSE WITNESS AGAINST YOUR NEIGHBOR.

X.
YOU SHALL NOT COVET YOUR NEIGHBOR'S HOUSE.

Moses and the Ten Commandments

© Demi 2025

Wisdom Tales in an imprint of World Wisdom, Inc.

Library of Congress Cataloging-in-Publication Data

Names: Hunt, Charlotte, author.
Title: Moses and the ten commandments / Demi.
Description: Bloomington : Wisdom Tales, [2025] | Audience: Ages 4-8 | Audience: Grades 2-3 | Summary: "The Bible tells us that "the Lord spoke to Moses face to face, as a man speaks to his friend" (Exodus 33:11). Born into captivity in Egypt, young Moses was hidden among the bulrushes of the Nile River to escape the sentence of death upon Hebrew infants. Discovered by the Pharoah's daughter, he was adopted by her and brought up in the royal palace. The Lord, however, would later instruct Moses to lead his people the Israelites out of slavery in Egypt, across the Red Sea, and into the Sinai Desert. And it was on Mount Sinai, amid thunder and lightning, fire and clouds of smoke, that the Lord would speak to Moses and reveal the Ten Commandments, which were "written with the finger of God" (Exodus 31:18) upon two tablets of stone. After wandering with his people in the desert for forty years, Moses would finally die on Mount Nebo, within sight of Canaan, the Promised Land. Award-winning author, Demi, recounts the dramatic story of Moses-prophet, liberator, and lawgiver to his people the Israelites"-- Provided by publisher.
Identifiers: LCCN 2024005164 (print) | LCCN 2024005165 (ebook) | ISBN 9781957670096 (hardback) | ISBN 9781957670102 (epub)
Subjects: LCSH: Moses (Biblical leader)--Juvenile literature. | Ten commandments--Juvenile literature. | BISAC: JUVENILE NONFICTION / Religion / Biblical Biography | JUVENILE NONFICTION / Religious / Christian / Early Readers
Classification: LCC BS580.M6 H86 2025 (print) | LCC BS580.M6 (ebook) | DDC 222/.16--dc23/eng/20240605
LC record available at https://lccn.loc.gov/2024005164
LC ebook record available at https://lccn.loc.gov/2024005165

Printed in China on acid-free paper

For information address Wisdom Tales,
P.O. Box 2682, Bloomington, Indiana, 47402-2682
www.wisdomtalespress.com

MOSES AND THE TEN COMMANDMENTS

DEMI

A round 1250 B.C. Moses was born in Egypt. The great pharaoh, Rameses II, feared the militant Hebrews and so ordered every Hebrew baby boy killed. Moses' mother hid him in a basket and floated him down the River Nile.

Moses grew up in the Egyptian palace as a prince. His mother, as a palace maid, secretly taught him his Hebrew heritage and sang to him songs of God.

One day Moses saw an Egyptian
strike a Hebrew worker.

Moses killed the Egyptian, but fearing
the Egyptians would kill him, he fled to
Midian in the Sinai wilderness.

While in the wilderness, God appeared
to Moses as flames of fire in a burning bush.

He told Moses to return to Egypt,
to free his people, and to bring
them to the promised land.

Moses followed the instructions
of God and returned to Egypt. He
asked the Pharaoh to let his people
go! But the Pharaoh refused.

God then helped Moses to free the
Hebrews by sending ten plagues:
turning the Nile River red with blood, frogs,
lice, flies, disease, boils, hail, locusts, darkness,
and the death of first-born Egyptians.

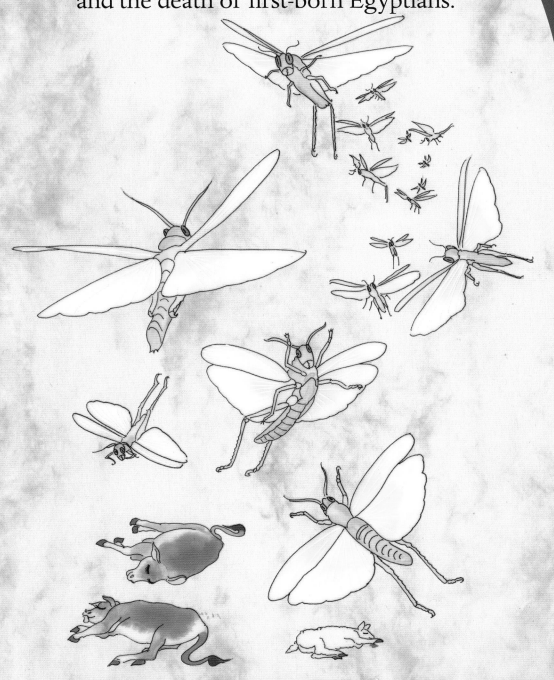

Furious, and defeated by the plagues,
the Pharaoh commanded Moses:

"Leave Egypt!"

Chased by the Egyptian army, Moses was helped
by God, who caused the Red Sea to part, killing
the Egyptian army but saving the Hebrews.

Then God led Moses into the Sinai
wilderness as a cloud by day,

and as a flame by night.

Then God called Moses to the top of Mount
Sinai and gave him the Ten Commandments
(Exodus 20:2-17):

I.
I AM THE LORD YOUR GOD, . . . YOU SHALL HAVE NO OTHER GODS BEFORE ME.

(Put God first)

II.
YOU SHALL NOT MAKE FOR YOURSELF A CARVED IMAGE.

(Worship God alone)

III.
YOU SHALL NOT TAKE
THE NAME OF THE LORD
YOUR GOD IN VAIN.

(Do not use God's Name disrespectfully)

IV.
REMEMBER THE SABBATH DAY, TO KEEP IT HOLY.

(Remember the day of the Lord)

V.
HONOR YOUR FATHER AND YOUR MOTHER.

(Respect your parents)

VI.
YOU SHALL NOT KILL.

(Do not harm other people)

VII.
YOU SHALL NOT COMMIT ADULTERY.

(Do not be unfaithful in marriage)

VIII.
YOU SHALL NOT STEAL.

(Do not take what belongs to others)

IX.
YOU SHALL NOT BEAR FALSE WITNESS AGAINST YOUR NEIGHBOR.

(Do not lie)

X.
YOU SHALL NOT COVET YOUR NEIGHBOR'S HOUSE.

(Do not seek after the possessions of others)

KEEP MY CO